I0221797

Nathaniel West

In Memory of Thomas Ebenezer Thomas

Delivered Sunday, March 14, 1875, in the First Presbyterian Church,

Dayton, Ohio

Nathaniel West

In Memory of Thomas Ebenezer Thomas
Delivered Sunday, March 14, 1875, in the First Presbyterian Church, Dayton, Ohio

ISBN/EAN: 9783337162139

Printed in Europe, USA, Canada, Australia, Japan

Cover: Foto ©Lupo / pixelio.de

More available books at **www.hansebooks.com**

IN MEMORY

OF

Thomas Ebenezer Thomas,

DELIVERED

Sunday, March 14, 1875, in the First Presbyterian Church, Dayton, Ohio.

BY

NATHANIEL WEST,

OF CINCINNATI.

Ἐκεῖνος ἦν ὁ λύχνος ὁ καιόμενος καὶ φαίνων.—John v. 35.

CINCINNATI:

ELM STREET PRINTING COMPANY, 176 & 178 ELM STREET.
1875.

AND is he gone, who brightly shone?
  Oh gloomy, gloomy night,
Here, left alone, we deeply moan
  His lost lamented light!
The Hero gone? the Prophet, too?
  Why does he cease to cry?
Oh, will not heaven the lamp renew?
  Say, did the Prophet die?

Discourse.

"And what shall I more say? for the time would fail me to tell of
Gideon, and Barak, and Samson, and Jephthah; David also, and
Samuel, and the prophets; who, through faith, subdued
kingdoms, wrought righteousness, obtained promises,
stopped the mouths of lions, quenched the violence
of fire, escaped the edge of the sword, out of
weakness were made strong, waxed valiant
in fight, turned to flight the armies of
the aliens."—Hebrews xi. 32–34.

CHOSEN to pronounce a commemorative address over
those whose valor had made them victims in the first
Peloponnesian war, and around whose public tomb
the cypress had begun to wave, Pericles thus spoke to
the assembled Athenians: "I deem it sufficient for
men who have approved their virtue in action, by action to be honored for it. Difficult it is judiciously
to handle a subject where even probable truth may not
gain assent in the minds of those who, through envy
of deeds which are beyond their own achievement,
pronounce all that is spoken to be exaggeration and
false. For the praises bestowed upon men are only to
be endured when others imagine they can do, them-

selves, those feats they hear to have already been
done."

By such words did the great orator express his judgment that " action," and not " oration," should sig-
nalize the tribute of a people's gratitude to those
whose lives had been made an offering for the public
welfare and glory. By such words did he give pre-
cedence to the long-drawn and solemnly-moving procession, the measured step, the trailing spears, the
drooping standards, the sumptuous funeral-car empty
in memory of the slain, the torch-light, the banquet,
and proud material monument, rather than to lamenta-
tions of mourners, orations pronounced, and elegaic
honors to the dead.

Reversely to this Pagan conception does the religion of Jesus teach us, that all mere outward and material demonstrations of regard for the meritorious
dead, are inferior to that better tribute which seeks to
perpetuate their virtues in lives conformed to their example, and in the enforcement and commendation of
the principles by which their actions were inspired and
adorned. " The righteous shall be in everlasting remembrance." " The memory of the just is blessed."
" Remember them who have rule over you, who have
spoken unto you the word of God, whose faith follow;
considering the end of their conversation, Jesus
Christ, the same yesterday, to-day, and forever."
" The teachers shall shine as the brightness of the
firmament; and they that turn many to righteousness,
as the stars forever and ever." Better than material
monument of Doric strength or Corinthian beauty,
than sarcophagus or mausoleum, where lie the ashes of
the dead inurned with funeral pomp, is that sublime
chapter of inspiration from which the words of the

text are taken. More than a Westminster Abbey, it is a Temple of Eternal Fame, wherein the names and deeds of heroes of the faith are recorded, and a niche left for the spiritual bust of every true successor in the line of their valor. To this Temple of Remembrance, built by the breath of the Holy Spirit, we come to-day. Its portals we enter. Here would we place our image, imperfect though it be, of him who was worthy, on earth, to stand beside " the elders " who, ages ago, " obtained a good report through faith," and who, now in heaven, stands crowned in their ranks, for ages to come, around the throne.

I am directed to the text because it presents an appropriate category wherein to class the name of one who so long was your honored pastor, lent of God not to you alone, but given to the whole Church, one who so long was a hero of the faith, a true soldier of Christ. Nor Gideon, nor Barak, nor Samson, nor Jephthah, nor David, nor Samuel, nor the prophets, held in higher regard the word of God, nor trusted with more unswerving fidelity to Him who had made it their absolute guide. Here lay the secret of his life and labors, trials and reproaches, courage, victories and unmurmuring death. Let the name of Thomas Ebenezer Thomas be inscribed upon the same tablet with the names of the judges, the prophets, the heroes, of Israel. To him, as to them, it was given, in high moral conflict, to subdue kingdoms, work righteousness, obtain promises, stop the mouths of lions, quench the violence of fire, escape the edge of the sword, out of weakness become strong, wax valiant in fight, turn to flight the armies of the aliens.

Shortly before his death it was my privilege, in company with another, to whom he was attached, to visit him just when his strength began to wane, and the tide of life to ebb slowly away. We found the soldier, wounded on the battlement, calmly reposing on his shield—"the shield of faith." Buckled tight to his head, and gleaming as ever, he still wore his helmet—"the helmet of salvation." Stretched on his shield, his hand supporting his weary head, his front glittered all over with " the breastplate of righteousness." Unsheathed by his side lay his well-tried sword, tested in many a conflict—"the sword of the Spirit, which is the word of God." Armed, *cap-a-pie*, with sandals on his feet, ready, faint as he was, either to walk " in the way of peace," or, if needs be, shout " the sword of the Lord and of Gideon," he seemed a very soldier, born and bred alike to the fortunes of holy war and the experience of rest that comes from victory. The pallor of his face and fading light in his eyes foreboded that the joy of his Lord, his eternal crown, was near. It was during the afternoon of Tuesday, February 2d, the winds from the hills moaned over the city of Cincinnati " *Dr. Thomas is dying!* " Pleuropneumonia was doing its fatal work. It was on the following morning of February 3d, the same winds moaned again, " *Dr. Thomas is dead!* " He had fallen asleep in Jesus. " And the voice said cry ! " And I said, " What shall I cry ? " And it said, " All flesh is grass, and all the goodliness thereof is as the flower of the field. The grass withereth, the flower fadeth, because the Spirit of the Lord bloweth upon it ; surely the people are grass ! The grass withereth, the flower fadeth, but the word of our God shall stand forever ! " " And I heard a voice from heaven saying unto me, *Write,* Blessed are the dead who die in the Lord from henceforth: *Yea, saith the Spirit,* that they may rest from their labors; and their works do follow them."

Doctor Thomas Ebenezer Thomas, eldest son of Rev. Thomas Thomas and Elizabeth Robinson, was of Welsh and English descent. The blood that flowed in the veins of a Christmas Evans, a John Elias, and a Howell Harris, gentle, fiery, chariot-like, and mounting, coursed in his own. The Puritan spirit that could welcome either martyrdom or exile, for righteousness' sake, and write a Smithfield, an Amsterdam, a Plymouth Rock, in its annals, was his. He was born in Chelmsford, England, December 23, 1812. While yet a child, but six years old, the decree of Him who led Israel through the sea wafted him across the Atlantic to find, in the New World, a theater of action for his boyhood, his manhood, his maturer age. With his parents he reached the shores of the United States, and landed at Baltimore in the year 1818. Together they journeyed to the city of Pittsburg, thence down the Ohio to Cincinnati. Prepared for college by his father, who himself was a graduate of Hoxton College, London, and a minister of the Independent Church, and whose " boarding-school " in the Miami country was the pride of its patrons, he was matriculated in Miami University in the fall of 1829, then under the supervision of President Bishop and Professors McGuffey, Scott, and Armstrong, and was graduated four years later, in the spring of 1834. Among his classmates and intimate friends were Rev. Dr. J. G. Monfort, Gov. Charles Anderson, Hon. W. S. Groesbeck, and others of eminent distinction.

Impressive incidents of his college life are still vivid in the memories of surviving companions. I pass by his reputation in debate and proficiency in scholarship, to mention but two. I have it from the testimony of an eminent servant of Christ, Dr. John M. Stevenson, of New York, that during his college course, Dr. Thomas fell into deep spiritual distress. "For weeks he was the special subject of prayer on the part of his pious fellow-students. He saw the truth of God's justice, and the criminality of sin, but could not see the infinite mercy of Christ as applied to his own soul. His chosen friends among the students prayed with him and for him, daily and nightly, rising at midnight to walk away into the grove with him to plead for the light of God's countenance." At length it came! "God brought him forth in the full and joyful experience of his love in Christ Jesus. From that time he became a bright, trustful, joyous, exultant Christian." He made a profession of his faith in Christ at Venice, Ohio, April 2, 1831, in the twentieth year of his age.

Remarkable was his moral heroism, as a youth, and his love of principle. Specially, as some yet remember, did it shine in face of danger, during the dreadful cholera scourge of 1833, when, resisting with a few others, the recalcitrant vote of his fellow-students, determined to abandon the University and seek refuge in flight, he remained firm to the last amid the despairing and the dying, thus supporting the hands of his instructors and receiving their warmest encomiums.

He was licensed at Oxford, Ohio, October, 1836, to preach the gospel. He was ordained to his first pastorate at Harrison, July, 1837, the period of the division of the Presbyterian Church into Old and New School. He became the pastor of the church at Hamilton, Ohio, in the fall of 1838. He was elected president of Hanover College in 1849, receiving his Doctorate from Wabash College in 1850, and resigned in 1854 to accept the Chair of Biblical Literature and Exegesis in the New Albany Theological Seminary, Indiana; increasing his burdens by discharging, also, the duties of the Professorship of Church History, and lecturing occasionally on Hermeneutics. A memorable crisis, well known to the Church, was at hand. The National Fugitive Slave Law had already been passed, and the struggle of the South for domination in the Church was intense as the battle for control in the government was violent. In 1852 the two great political parties of the country had pronounced the Fugitive Slave Law a " finality."

General Assemblies and Halls of Congress echoed to each other in fiery debate. In 1857 the nine Western and Northwestern Synods, associated in the conduct of New Albany Seminary, removed it to Chicago, Illinois, and in 1858 offered its control, as a measure of peace and prosperity, to the General Assembly, expecting that the antislavery sentiment of the Northwest would be regarded in any new organization of the institution the Assembly might make. To evince the perfect sincerity of this offer, the argument then being that all Theological Seminaries should be under Assembly control, directly and immediately, Dr. Thomas and his distinguished colleague, Rev. E. D. MacMaster, D. D., resigned their professorships. As the reward of their magnanimity, both were laid aside by the dominant Southern sentiment in the General Assembly of 1859, met at Indianapolis. The civil war was rapidly approaching. Meanwhile Dr. Thomas remained in New Albany, as stated supply to the Presbyterian Church in that place. In 1858 he was called to the pastorate of the First Presbyterian

Church, Dayton, Ohio, there to remain, in the providence of God, until the issues of the contest of three generations had been solved in a nation's blood, and the sundered branches of the Presbyterian Church reunited. In 1871 he was elected to the Chair of New Testament Greek and Exegesis, in Lane Theological Seminary, supplying the pulpit, also, in the Broadway Presbyterian Church, Cincinnati, and the pulpit at Walnut Hills, near the Seminary. In the fourth year of his labors in Lane Seminary, a voice called to him from above, " Well done, good and faithful servant ! " " Come up hither ! " The silver cord was loosed, the golden bowl was broken, the pitcher at the fountain, the wheel at the cistern ! The dust returned to the earth as it was, and the spirit to God who gave it.

> " Welcome, the hour of full discharge,
> That set his longing soul at large,
> Unbound his chain, broke up his cell,
> And gave him with his God to dwell."

The measure of Dr. Thomas' professional life may, therefore, be thus divided : 1. Two years of academic teaching at Rising Sun, Indiana, and Franklin, Ohio, subsequent to his graduation and previous to his licensure, i. e., from 1834 to 1836. 2. Five years of Presidency in Hanover College, i. e., from 1849 to 1854. 3. Twenty-seven years of active and successful pastoral and pulpit work : in Harrison from 1836 to 1839 ; in Hamilton from 1839 to 1849; in New Albany from 1857 to 1858; in Dayton from 1858 to 1871; besides his pulpit labors in Cincinnati and at Walnut Hills. 4. Seven years of devoted toil in the Professor's Chair, in New Albany, from 1857 to 1859, in Lane Seminary from 1871 to 1875. In all *forty years* of active Christian life, as a public instructor, in the school, the college, the seminary, the pastorate ; training the faculties and molding the manners of the young, instilling the principles of virtue and religion, proclaiming the unsearchable riches of Christ, resisting manfully the encroaching and overspreading corruptions in Church and State in their common subserviency to a system of human oppression rich with the spoil of unnumbered souls, thrilling the fibers of the human frame with magnetic and matchless eloquence, in Presbytery, Synod, and Assembly, from platform and sacred desk alike, and pressing on to the goal, not counting his life dear, determined that Christ should be magnified in his body, whether by life or by death !

As a man, physically, Dr. Thomas was of medium stature, strong in constitution, solidly built, and of fair complexion. His voice was feeble yet possessed of unusual charm. On his shoulders he bore a " dome of thought " seldom seen on the shoulders of men. On the wall of that " palace " fancy hung her pictures wrought in colors of striking beauty, and high intellectual lights threw their splendor over the scene within. He was clear in understanding, comprehensive in grasp, quick and penetrating in perception. Affable in manners, accessible and courteous, manly and dignified, tender as a child, sympathetic and tearful, free, frank, generous, firm when firmness was needed, playful as a sportive jet from the fountain, mirthful with his keen twinkling eye, sparkling with anecdote, wit and humor, and chaste in every expression, he was one of the most socially gifted, delightful, and companionable of men. Enthusiastic in hospitality, who that knocked at his door and felt the warm grasp of his hand could ever forget that hearty welcome : " Come in, thou blessed

of the Lord ; wherefore standest thou without ? "
Resolute in will and of tenacious purpose, forming his
judgment without prejudice, yet amenable to persuasion and honest argument, uncompromising in principle, respectful and magnanimous to the last degree, a
man without the shadow of personal resentment or desire of personal revenge, he was just such a friend as
the high-souled and noble among men delighted to
cultivate and honor. Ardent in temperament and im-
pulsive, because strung with the finest sensibilities of
soul added to quickness of natural perception, intense
in his moral convictions, delicate as a maid, yet brave
as a lion and regardless of self, his soul sprang, as by
a single leap, to the side of the right, and triumphed
or fell with the cause it espoused. His courage remained undaunted by misfortune. His confidence was
unbroken by adversity. His righteousness sustained
him. His presence was a tower of strength to any
cause. If, at times, the ardor of virtue betrayed him
into verbal indiscretions, which, in calmer moods, his
better judgment would have shunned, none read-
ier than he to ask forgiveness. He seemed born to
hate meanness, injustice, oppression, and insolent of-
fending. To malice his heart was a stranger. Secret
calumny found no arrows in his tongue with which to
shoot, privily, at his neighbor. Crawling circumven-
tion, sanctimonious and soft-footed intrigue, vainly
concealing the envy that bore murder in its purpose,
shrewd cunning, silent and sly, duplicity, stratagem,
plot, craft, trick, treachery, slander, and the hollow
smile of simulated friendship, the whole brood of moral
abominations, his manly soul abhorred. On all he
wrote " *Anathema.*"

" From the loud roar of foaming calumny,
To the small whisper of the as paltry few,
And subtler venom of the reptile crew,
The Janus glance of whose significant eye,
Learning to lie with silence, would *seem* true,
And, without utterance, save the shrug or sigh,
Deal round to happy fools its speechless obloquy."

Better moral metal never was found in man. He was the soul of honor, integrity and truth.

But these virtues of his character, bright as they were, stood inferior to other adornments, whose luster outshone the gems that Aaron wore. Throughout the whole wealth of his genius, lively or grave, morally stern or socially flexible, spirituality and sanctity marked him as their own. The cross of Christ had subdued him. The Spirit of Christ had anointed him. He had studied his Master, as Harris in his " Great Teacher " had studied Him. The contrast between himself and Christ was vivid in his consciousness, and this made him humble. At times an inward glance at Christ would check the playfulness of his mood and tone him into saintly thoughtfulness. To be like Christ—this was his aim. To battle with the corruptions of his sinful nature and emerge victorious from the contest—this was his inward agony and prayer. To despair of self and find strength and peace in looking alone to Christ—this was his daily experience. It explained all his spiritual states. He made one thing clear as sunshine—the fact that he had not one spiritual grace which did not come to him through faith in Christ. He saw in Christ all that he needed, and by looking, obtained it. Christ's humility made him humble ; Christ's poverty, patience, sanctity, tenderness, love and zeal, made him poor, patient, saintly, tender, loving and zealous.

Christ's intercession made him prayerful. What he had of grace he received by "looking unto Jesus." The Holy Spirit wrought through Christ, upon his soul, and not outside of, nor apart from Christ. All the spiritual light he ever enjoyed came, as he said, "through Christ." Christ was the miracle, the magnet, the mystery of his life.

The piety of Dr. Thomas was not morbid. It was fresh as the dew of Hermon, bright as the glow of the morning. It was not self-generated. It came from above. Fervor and exhilarating life were in it, a power as when some new emotion kindles the soul for the first time. The supernatural grafted itself upon the natural, and yet the individuality of the man was not lost in the sanctification of the saint. A quality of tenderness, too, full of persuasion and sweetness, made it all the more precious. Trials had ministered, through grace, to cast over it, at times, the tinge of sadness. He had drank something of the cup his Master drank; entered, in some measure, into the deep mysteries of his Master's sufferings and reproach. Gethsemanes, Calvarys, and dark eclipses of the spirit, though brief, visited him during the trying struggle of practical obedience, in public life, to his Father's will. No theme touched his pious affections more deeply than the mention of his Master's name. The fountain and the flame were close together in his heart, neither to extinguish nor destroy the other, but the one to burn, the other to bedew, and both to bless. Well do I remember, as one day we sat beneath the trees near his study, the theme of our conversation was the "Redeemer's Tears." I asked him if ever he had noticed Luther's beautiful version of the text "Jesus wept" —"the eyes of Jesus go over." He said nothing, but

looking steadfastly in my face—just as a river swells
to its banks, or the water to the goblet's brim, and
overflows, so did the moisture gather in his eyes, and
breaking over their lids, already too full to hold more,
ran down in pious streams upon his cheeks !

His love for the word of Christ, not less than for his
Master, was remarkable. He panted for it as the hart
for the water-brooks ; cried for it as the hungering
sheep for the green meadows. Morning by morning
his Divine Shepherd wakened his ear to hear as the
learned. While yet his family were locked in slumber,
he would rise, and, opening the shutters to the dawn,
gaze with delight upon the dew-gemmed pastures of
the Hebrew Psalter he loved so well. Margin on margin, fly-leaves and covers, from beginning to end, two
copies of the Psalter in the original tongue, are marked with expressions of his affectionate pleasure and
care. At midnight, too, he would rise to record with
his pen the verses his whispering heart had indited.
Blessed man ! Planted by the river of water, fruit-
bearing not only in season, but out of season, his leaf
never withering ! And well did he know how to
minister consolation to the afflicted. The Lord God
had given him " the tongue of the learned that he
should know how to speak a word in season to him
that is weary." Sorrow found in him a comforter at her
couch, not less than did joy a guest at her banquet. The
humility that shone transparent through the vesture of
his strength was no mere natural modesty. It was the
feature of a spirit molded by Christ, penitent under a
sense of its own unworthiness, conscious of its eternal
indebtedness to the mercy and love of Jesus, chastened
by trials with which his Master had honored and tested
him, and confirmed by a felt need of it, "lest he should

be exalted above measure by the abundance of the revelations given to him."

Shall I speak of his faith? From the hour it pleased God to reveal his Son in him, and give him victory over law and conscience, doubt, fear, and self-condemnation, and bring him forth to the enlargement of spiritual liberty, he was a buoyant, joyful, trustful disciple. Simple, spirit-born, and unfaltering was this bright particular star in the constellation of his graces. It was in him a conviction deeper than granite foundations, loftier than the firmament, outlasting the limits of an earthly career. It was the faith of Gideon and Barak, and Samson and Jephthah. Not Gibraltar, impervious to attack, nor the rocky sides of Ehrenbreitstein, were to be compared to God in Christ, his Strength, his Rock, his Fortress, his High Tower, his Deliverer. It was, to him, an inwrought certain persuasion and assurance, an unshakable conviction and clinching proof of the reality of things hoped for, though yet unseen. Once, in company with a friend, I asked him if, in his definition of faith, he agreed with Calvin, that it is a " certain knowledge " in the soul that God in Christ is propitious to me, and that Christ is mine. He replied, " Faith is a conscious confidence—a cable—*pistis*. Since my first confidence in Christ, having passed through great conflict, I have never entertained a doubt of my interest in Him, nor of His in me!" How modestly he spake it! " It is sinful," said he, " to doubt. My spiritual state has often troubled me, but I have never doubted Christ's interest in me since I believed." To the question of Rev. Dr. Skinner, " Dr. Thomas, to what do you attribute this assurance of which you speak? Is it to any special revelation you have of Christ's love to you, or to any miraculous work of the Spirit, different from what others enjoy, or to any moods or frames of mind, or sense of your own perfection, or anything whatever you find in yourself?" His answer was, "To nothing of the kind. I attribute my assurance to Christ's promise and to my confidence in Christ alone. They are the same thing. Christ is a sure foundation. I can't trust my frames or my heart, but I can trust Christ. Of course, faith is the Spirit's work, yet it is I who believe." Such was his reply. Christ, in His objective fullness, was his all.

A Christian moralist, he accepted the commandment of God as the ultimate rule for himself and for others. He affirmed its empire over every passion, every human interest and will. Duty to God and duty to man were, in his view, the condition of all social, civil and ecclesiastical progress, and the discharge of it the essence of all virtue. He denied to any man the right to set aside the precept of God, under any pretense whatever, no matter how plausible. Theory with him was practice. The wretched utilitarian maxim of Paley, so common in our day—"that what is expedient is right"—so grounding our obligation to speak and act, upon our own opinions and personal inclinations, interests and moods, he repudiated as treason to God, as the overthrow of all morality, the source of immeasurable moral corruption. As to the mode of discharging what God requires, he admitted room for diversity of view, but done must the duty be, at all hazards and regardless of all consequences. Righteousness must be asserted and maintained in every relation of life, social, civil, religious, at whatever cost. The oily appeal to "the prudential motive" that slips through all God's commandments, balances advantage against disadvantage, makes public or private opinion the censor of the divine word, and does obeisance to conscience only when civil statute and sheriff are near to enforce obligation, or when individual and clique interests are promoted, the morality that winks at sin and the concealment of sin for the sake of peace and prosperity and hope of God's glory, and degrades conscience itself to a plaything to be bartered and sold in the market, he scorned. Its practice awoke the moral antagonism of his whole soul. To his mind, Christian virtue was impossible without Christian manliness and courage, because we ourselves are sinful, and live in a world of sin. It gave grandeur and power to all his private and public acts. Whether in Church or State, in private or public, the choice between a corrupt peace or a righteous war was neither doubtful nor difficult. He had enlisted under Christ whom, alone, he called "Master." Injustice, oppression, perversion of God's truth, or God's way, in any form, could not be where he dwelt, and not hear his indignant protest, or receive his well-delivered blow. In his catechism of right and wrong, the high behests of Heaven were not human calculations of temporal profit and loss, inconvenience and ease, but " the dictates of a lip divine," whose every word is law. It was not merely the shame, but as well the damage and personal demoralization, consequent upon the violation of Christian morality, that made it so odious in his sight. For, in the nobility of his spirit, he judged that where the dignity of virtue ceases to attract the praises of men, and compromises and expediencies prevail to usurp divine rules—when conscience is strangled by the prescript of a truckling neutrality, disgraceful as corrupting, then that which ennobles the Christian man and gives him royalty and state among men, and praise with God, is forever lost. The victory of the Christian soldier is betrayed. The vision of virtue fades from the Christian consciousness, Christian integrity has perished, and man, despoiled of the enchantment that would guide his steps —through suffering indeed—to glory, sinks to the level of a base trimmer, venal to the highest bidder who pollutes his hands with his purchase. The negative morality of neutrality and expediency becomes, whether in personal or public relations, an Italian stab, an indirect assassination.

Not such were the models of Dr. Thomas. Careless what men objected, if only God approved, and willing to face the intrenched carnal expediency of the hour, the ideals he placed before him as aids to inspire his purpose were Socrates before the judges, Elijah before Ahab, John the Baptist before Herod, Stephen before the Sanhedrim, Paul before Felix and Agrippa, Luther before Pope and Emperor. Such, also, were Knox before Mary, Melville before James, and, more than all, his own Master before Caiaphas and Pilate! If there is any one trait of character in which he, to whose memory we bring this tribute to-day, looms in honor before the Church and the nation, it is the grandeur of his moral integrity. To every servant of fear, advising retreat from the presence of danger, his answer was, "Go tell thy Lord, Behold Elijah is here!" or "Go tell that fox, Behold, I cast out devils, and do cures to-day and to-morrow, and the third day I shall be perfected."

In all that enters into the institution of a Christian scholar, Dr. Thomas was eminent and accomplished. This testimony is confirmed by all his pupils and friends, not a few of whom occupy eminent positions in Church and State to-day. During his curriculum, he excelled as a student and gave promise of coming distinction. His love of study remained to the last. To history, biography, poetry, botany, geology, ethnology and entomology, he gave attention as his more pressing duties permitted. He was a library in himself. Shelves were in his capacious memory, laden with volumes of solid learning, the lore of ancient and modern times; cabinets, too, of scientific treasure. English and American, as well as Greek and Roman classics, were there, antiquarian research, the best criticism of the age in his own department, ethics and theology—all to enjoy and use for the benefit of his fellow-man. His choice, however, was the study of language and the interpretation of the Sacred Scriptures. He had seen, in early life, over the thorns of his crucified Master, an inscription written in characters of "Hebrew, Greek and Latin." These consecrated tongues he made his own. Not less a Protestant than Christian, he believed, as Luther did, that "it is a part of religion to learn and teach Hebrew and Greek." The Reformation, he contended, rested on that fact, and he was the sworn foe of Popery. No number of modern languages, however useful or admired, could justify, in his view, the neglect of Hebrew and Greek. The " Magna Charta of Christianity and the Church," he said, " is in them." The tongues of Paris and Berlin are not so much as to be compared with those of Athens, Jerusalem and Rome. Enthusiastic in the classics, he viewed them as the best basis of the best culture, better than discipline in any or all the natural sciences together. The Latin he could speak and write with ease. He preferred the Greek. By the

study of their faultless models, his naturally gifted and
susceptible mind became trained to that discrimination
of thought, crystal clearness and perfection of style,
exquisite taste, beauty of illustration, elegance, direct-
ness and force of expression, which characterized his
own. How deeply he drank of the " Pierian Spring!"
How often the allusion adorned his diction ! How fre-
quently, even in religious discussions, his speech was
graced with sentiments drawn directly from the clas-
sic fountains ! another insatnce that sacred eloquence
and prayer alike have flowed from lips

" Wet with Castalian dews ! "

He was even more devoted to Hebrew than' Greek.
He understood perfectly the genius and laws of the
language. He loved it, moreover, chiefly because of its
contents. He could repeat Psalms and sections of the
Prophets without difficulty. It was not for mere literary amusment, however, he loved the study of the languages. A nobler motive spurred him to their diligent
pursuit. It was to be able to reach with certainty, for
himself, the heart of divine truth; to open and pass
through " the nearest doors to the mind of the Spirit;"
to be able to serve God with his best powers, and to
sow seed for eternal life. His last effort was a re-
translation of the celebrated epistle to Diognetus, and
an argument built thereupon to prove in opposition to
modern infidel schools of criticism,' how deeply the
very words of the gospels had sunk into the hearts of
the Christian Church in the beginning of the second
century.

As a theologian, Dr. Thomas was Calvinistic to the
core. He was familiar with some of the Church
fathers and with the great Calvinistic divines of the

Reformation. He had studied Calvin and Beza, Van Mark and DeMoor, Witsius and Martyr, Turrettin and Stapfer. His favorites among the English theogians were Flavel and Baxter, Howe, Owen and Bates, Manton and Charnock. Liberal in spirit, because loving the truth in its fullness, overleaping the boundaries of his own denomination in his Christian regards, and unfettered by extremes of whatever school, he had no sympathy with those who, ever professing to be orthodox, are yet ever complaining of the difficulties of their creed, and sighing for theological nurses to spoon out "milk" to babes rather than for well instructed scribes to divide "strong meat" to men. Creed-tinkerers he regarded as superficial and incompetent. He loved the Gideons and Baraks in theology, an Athanasius, an Augustine, a Luther, a Calvin, who had "earnestly contended for the faith once delivered to the saints." If the Church creed had, in any degree, become what some would call a "dead orthodoxy," it was not the fault of the creed, but of the men who professed it for the glory of its historic name, and yet preferred to it some new, unhistoric, and piebald actualism, unlike any compound ever put up before! Upon this point his mind was precisely expressed by the celebrated Dr. Chalmers in a quotation which, years ago, he told me John Angell James had inserted in his "Earnest Ministry." I have not only no reason to believe that Dr. Thomas ever changed his opinion in this respect, but positive reasons to the contrary. The quotation is from a publication of Dr. Chalmers, about the time of the disruption of the Scotch Establishment and organization of the Free Church: "We do not need to take down the framework of our existing orthodoxy. All we require is that

it shall become an animated frame-work, by the breath
of a new life infused into it. What we want is that the
very system of doctrine, we now have, shall come to
us, not in word only but in power. Prayer can bring
this about." Dr. Thomas learned his theological system, however, not from text-books or scholastic man-
uals, although he was an able theologian, and the com-
panion of the greatest theologian in the West, but
from the Bible alone. Here was his forte. Interrogated
once in the following manner: "Dr. Thomas, where
did you get your theology?" he responded, "I
found it in the Bible." "I meant," said the interrogator, "who was your theological teacher?" "My chief
theological preceptor," said he, "was Professor Paul,
who was brought up at the feet of Professor Gamaliel,
and my judgment is that he was a better teacher than
his master." "Ah, yes!" replied the interrogator,
"but I was inquiring in what seminary you were
trained?" "I never saw a theological seminary," answered Dr. Thomas, "until after I was ordained." It
was not that he undervalued seminary instruction, but
only that Providence had prepared him for the ministry
without it. But he had done what few do in the course
of that preparation. He had passed into the heart of
the sacred originals. He had made himself a first-
class competent judge of Bible doctrine, able for himself to tell what system is true, what system is false.
The form of doctrine he adopted was eminently biblical, and the spirit of that form was, to his mind, expressed as well in the Calvinistic symbols as it could
be. He was no innovator. In the language of his
colleague, Professor Evans, of Lane Seminary, "The
Bible was to him, in a very earnest sense, his supreme
and sole authority in faith and practice." Catholic in

his creed as could any one be who is evangelical, he was yet conservative of the old dogmatic truths. Scripture for him was not a quarry where every man might chip and square the stones to suit the necessities of some preconceived theory of his own, but a deposit of sacred truth, already fitted, stone to stone, for the heavenly temple, yet scattered about in different places, without system, and for the wisest purposes. The utmost any system could do, in his judgment, is to approximate the complete conception of the relation and harmony of the different parts in the temple of inspired truth, not fully to compass them. And yet, as between the two great opposing systems of theology which have perpetuated the conflict of ages—the one starting with the principle of divine agency and continuing with it throughout, operating in man the initial as well as continuous and final work of grace, and the other, starting with the principle of human agency and only introducing the divine as supplementary and synergistic, so making the work of grace conditioned on human co-operation—he declared, unhesitatingly, for the former. He held it to be the only true, only possible and non-contradictory conception of *grace*, in the very nature of the case, one postulate being admitted, viz: the "death in sin" of the whole human race. Of this "death in sin" and utter spiritual ruin, God had given him deep personal experience, and on the other hand a triumphant confidence in the salvation that is in Christ. He repudiated the conclusion that because Scripture propositions are not formulated in an ecclesiastical creed, therefore they are not dogmatic. He affirmed them to be more dogmatic than any creed could make them and of higher authority. Creeds he admitted. They were to him *mensuræ mensuratæ*—rules ruled—but the Bible *mensura men-surans*, the rule ruling. His genius gave him a predilection for the grandeur of divine mysteries. To destroy these, by foolish explanations, is to rifle the Bible of the signs the most elementary of its origin. Mountain, ocean, and mine, were the playthings of his childhood. He was ready to confess that God had made *him*, and not he *God*. He had sense enough to admit that the music of the ocean is impossible without its depths, the flowers of earth without its rock-ribbed foundations, the glitter of the firmament without immensity behind it. And so did he say that the simplest truths of the Bible are impossible without the underlying deep things in the dazzling abyss of His bosom to whom no man has ever been counselor. He remembered " God answered Job out of a whirlwind " and scattered his puny objections to the mysteries of the divine administration, as chaff is scattered before the tempest, by a simple reference, in the physical domain, to the mysteries of Arcturus and Mazzaroth, Pleiades and Orion, Behemoth, "who moveth his tail like a cedar," and Leviathan, "who maketh the deep to boil as a pot." He loved Paul's ejaculation, " O the depths!" and said amen to Calvin's motto, "Let God be true and every man a liar.'

If the consistent voice of pupils, colleagues, directors, and those who best knew him, is of value, Dr. Thomas stood second to none as a teacher in the Presbyterian Church, or in the nation. The rich furniture of his mind, the sharpness of his intuition, his power of induction and deduction, his logical precision and comprehensive grasp, his exhaustive treatment and ability to impart instruction to others, ranked him as an educator of the first degree. He exercised a stimulating effect on the minds of his students. As President, he commanded respect and obedience, as Professor, an attachment that was simply romantic. The chair of instruction was his throne. No clod, cold and lifeless, was there, burdened by a sense of its own importance, while he sat in it. The scholar was smitten with the enthusiasm of the master, the pupil with the charm of the teacher. He connected every student with himself by wires of his own battery, and a magnetic stream of sympathy ran tingling through them all. Sometimes a shock and a flash might indeed wake the disciple to a sense of his responsibilities, but not oftener than beads of dew might be seen in the Master's eyes. Only the genius of an adept in the art could guide the steps of the learner, without weariness, through intricate processes of argument and exposition. "As a teacher," says Dr. Scovel, of Pittsburg, who sat at his feet for seven years, "he was unsurpassed. In the quiet summer afternoons, during his presidency, with the audience of young men seated solidly in front of him, with Robinson's Greek Harmony in his hand, and a section of the Life of Christ under review, I have known him to hold the students and the audience an hour and a half, and leave them hungering for more. He could not but be fervent, who thought so clearly and felt so deeply." Says the Rev. Dr. Stevenson, of New York, "His love for truth was conspicuous and unvarying, his enthusiasm and skill in imparting to his students, whether collegiate or theological, his wealth of knowledge. were equaled only by his ability to set them upon independent lines of study for themselves. In all these respects he stood peer to the unsurpassed Dr. E. D. MacMaster, his dearly loved associate and brother in New Albany Seminary." It is the affirmation of one of the most judicious among the students of Lane Seminary, " There is not a young man in the Seminary who would not prefer losing his dinner rather than one of Dr. Thomas' lectures." If love of truth and hatred of all superficiality—if skill to attach and lift the meanest intellect to unexpected heights, and animate it with the apprehension of hope —if success in rousing the mind from indolent and passive sequacity to independent and active advance, and inspiring it with confidence of its own attempts—if to blend the severe and the tender, authority with affection, the sparkle of wit with sober demeanor, insuring obedience, respect, proficiency, and love—if to infuse the life of his pupils with Christian manliness, integrity of purpose, nobility of character, and the spirit of a lofty aim—if, above all, to fix in their souls that Christ, and Christ alone, is the only object worth living for— if these things are the marks of a prince among teachers, then he who has gone to gaze on the face of the "Great Teacher" forever, has left none behind to dispute his eminence in the qualifications we have named. Hundreds of young men, both in and out of the Presbyterian Church, are the fruit of his faithful labors and prayers, some of whom have gone peacefully to their rest, or " fallen asleep " fighting for their country on the ensanguined field.

Shall I speak of him as a preacher and pastor? How imperfect must be my poor utterance in presence of you who, for thirteen years, listened with delight to his instructions and were the objects of his spiritual care! The Christian pastorate was to him an awful function. Its honor scarce compensated for its solemn responsibility. He regarded it as more noble than the Aaronic priesthood. God, eternity, man, sin and salvation, are its themes. Yet nature and grace alike had qualified him for the pulpit and given him that combination of endowments, richness of knowledge and spiritual unction, which contributed so highly to the life and vigor of his discourse. He stood, the ornament of the sacred desk. Notwithstanding the feebleness of his voice,

He had Elijah's dignity of tone,
And all the love of the beloved John.

"He was a burning and shining light." He shone with no doubtful splendor. Sensationalism and mechanical revivalism found in him no support. The light he brought to the pulpit was no fancy blue and green, no gaslight, nor torchlight, nor tallow flame, but heaven's own sunlight, unclouded, brilliant and pure. It was "Christ, the Light of the World," he held up before blinded men. If he scorched the Pharisees, as did John the Baptist and the Master himself, it was not a hissing rocket he let off, no display of Greek fire, but the focal concentration, "in the spirit and power of Elias," of the truth of God, through the Scripture lens, that made the conscience smoke and burn. And yet who more tender? Who more tearful, in or out of the pulpit? Was it not the stern Baptist who said, "Behold the Lamb of God which taketh away the sin of the world?" Was it not Jesus who wept on Olivet after the thunder of his denunciations had reverberated in the temple? Even such was the case with our departed. His felicity in expounding the text or chapter, as the case might be, his exhaustive analysis and presentation of the most difficult passages so clearly that the simplest intellect might understand as well as the profoundest admire, checked not the flow of his tenderest emotions, nor the outburst of his sanctified fire. Where will you find a tongue more persuasive? Who that heard his exposition of the psalm, "My God, my God, why hast thou forsaken me?" or his sermon on the text, "The love of Christ constraineth us," or hundreds of others of pathetic appeal, can ever forget the warm glow and the streaming tenderness of his address? It was in the heat of one of the most violent political contests ever known, that during a meeting of the Synod of Cincinnati, one of his strongest opponents, now with him in glory, a man eminent on the bench, heard him preach the sacramental sermon before the Synod. With tears running down his cheeks, he approached, at the close, to grasp the hand of the preacher he had never grasped before, and said, with faltering voice, "Dr. Thomas, we are one forever!" O blessed, blessed Spirit, who thus endowedst thy servant to preach the unsearchable riches of Christ, and break through the barriers of the strongest prejudice! And you, who have marked his pathos and communion with God, on sacramental occasions, when now he would gather you around the cross, and now would lead you to the mount of transfiguration, where his devotions overflowed, how can you forget his tenderness and love! As one has well said, what "a fragrant blossoming of study, thought, experience, and glowing love to God and man!" None realized more than he, as he moved among you, his own insufficiency. He knew that only the power that cleaves the sea and breaks the rocks could convert a soul—and knowing this, how often he spake as a dying man to dying men, and prayed how fervently! All pomp and affectation he abhorred. His aim was not self-presentation, but the presentation of Christ, the conversion and edification

of souls, and the Christian walk and life of his people.
Here, to this flock, for thirteen years he preached,

> In language plain,
> And plain in manner, decent, solemn, chaste,
> And natural in gesture; much impressed
> Himself, as conscious of his awful charge
> And anxious, mainly, that the flock he fed
> Might feel it too. Affectionate in look,
> And tender in address, as well becomes
> A messenger of grace to guilty men.

Eloquence to him was only a vehicle by which, not
shunning to declare the whole counsel of God, he be-
sought, persuaded, entreated, and prayed men to be
reconciled to God. His human models were a Newton, a Cecil, a Baxter, a Bunyan, a Whitfield, an Evans,
a Harris, a Flavel and McCheyne—but, more than all,
he drew his inspiration from a Paul and John, and
most from the Master himself. Everywhere, at Harrison, Hamilton, New Albany, Dayton, Cincinnati and
Walnut Hills, he was held in the admiration, reverence
and love of his people. The fruit of his ministry was
extensive and precious. Eternity alone will reveal
the number of souls to whom it was a blessing.

This magnificent edifice, erected to the worship of
God by your beneficence and his unwearied persistence
and resolution, stands a monument of his indomitable
enthusiam, public spirit, and pastoral zeal. He was the
last man on earth to put God off with mean things.
Like the sainted Dr. Edward Andrews, of Walworth,
England, he could answer every objector by the short
argument, " God, my boy, should be worshiped with
the very best of everything—best architecture, best
painting, best organ, best music, best singing, best
poetry, best preaching, best genius, best people. He

gave us Jesus, the best he had to give. Shall we not give him our best in return?"

Dr. Thomas was an orator without a superior in the Presbyterian Church, and unsurpassed outside of it. Had he possessed the voice some men possess, a world-wide fame had been his. But oratory consists neither of declamation, nor artistic elocution, nor vocal force. The throat of a Stentor could not make it, nor could all the arts of a mere rhetorical accomplishment create it. But if a worthy cause, a virtuous character, a clear conception outrunning tedious deduction, a noble end, sympathy with righteousness, and forgetfulness of self; if logical precision kindling into intense emotion, truthful utterance, amplitude of illustration and beauty of diction; if force of imagination, tact of approach, readiness of anecdote and wit, dignity and deliberation, relieved by fervor and grace of bodily action and gesture, with emphasis always in the right place—if these are the essentials of an orator, then Dr. Thomas was second to none in the whole land. We judge, by the rule of Cicero, that eloquence is simply " Wisdom speaking fluently," or by the rule of Quintilian, that three things mark the orator, " He instructs, he moves, he delights;" or by the rule of Augustine, " Matters of small moment are to be spoken lowly, those of ordinary importance temperately, and great things grandly and fluently;" or by the rule of the gifted Fenelon, " The orator speaks naturally; he speaks not as a declaimer; things flow from the fountain; his utterances are living and full of movement. The heat that animates him gives birth to expressions and figures he could never have fashioned in his study." And judged by such canons as these from the writings of men who have given oratorical law to the world, Dr. Thomas deserved a place beside the best orators of ancient or modern times. Difficult at times to hear his voice, yet, when roused to its clear strength and impelled by the ardor that bore him along, unconscious of his power, his accents streamed through the souls of men as magnetic currents stream, and flamed as the lightning flames! It was not literally true that he made "each particular hair stand on end." It *was*, however, true, that at times, not a few of the vast audience *thought* so. Concluded—every fiber trembling with emotion—he sat down amid the applauses of an enraptured audience whose pulses throbbed high with excitement, and whose unrestrained admiration of the speaker broke out in redoubling, and, one would think, unending demonstrations. He had the fire of Demosthenes, the diction of Tully. Like the elder Scaliger, he touched nothing he did not adorn—"*nil tetigit quod non ornavit*." He was greater than Spurgeon, greater than Cumming, greater than Parsons or Monod, in the breadth of his accomplishments, in the loftiness of his intellect, in the brilliancy of his genius, in the impassioned outbursts of his sympathies, in the eloquence of his tongue. In his best moods, Patrick Henry and Chatham would have been proud of him. It affords me great pleasure to repeat to you here the testimony of one of your own journals, in support of this tribute to his oratorical powers. Speaking of your loved pastor, it said: "During his residence in Dayton his influence on all great public occasions was invoked, and he always gave to any cause with which he co-operated great strength, and that which he opposed was apt to break down under his frown. Whatever he touched with his golden speech blazed with beauty. His delivery was fiery and impassioned, though very graceful. His language, which flowed from his eloquent lips in a limpid, unbroken volume, always seemed to fit the place into which it fell, as exactly as if he had deliberately measured and calculated all the proportions and conditions. He knew by intuition exactly what to say on most occasions, and precisely how to say it. the most effectively. As an Englishman would say, he knew wonderfully well how to 'put things.' Logic and fancy seemed so admirably balanced in his mind that you were apt to consider his speeches perfect. Among the notable speeches of his life, in Dayton, were his splendid Thanksgiving Sermon, in 1863, when he chose the Feast of Purim, described in Esther, for his text, and his thrilling half-hour speech in the Court House on the day of the assassination of President Lincoln—*an involuntary burst of eloquence that never was exceeded by any orator.*"—*Dayton Journal*, February 4, 1875.

The criticism is just. Search the denominations where you will, go to the State Legislatures or your halls of Congress, the peer of Dr. Thomas as an orator is scarcely to be found. Dayton has a right to be proud of him. The Church is proud of him. In vain—in vain—will this people and this community seek to fill his place. It can not be filled! Chrysostom had the·golden mouth, Augustine the flaming heart, Calvin the conception and conviction of moral righteousness—our brother, gone to glory, had them all!

I should be guilty of injustice to the rare gifts with which God endowed our departed brother, did I not mention among them his poetic talent. Could a heart so warm, a taste so exquisite, a sense of harmony and love of music so strong, a facility of expression, genius, and imagination, such as he had, fail to utter themselves at times in verse? Impossible! Many are his productions of this kind, and of the first literary merit. It will be a great loss, if these, in company with his lectures, orations, and sermons, are not given to the Church in whose bosom he sparkled as a gem. His lyrics prove him worthy of the bays that twined around the brows of Montgomery and Watts, Cowper and Newton, Wesley and McCheyne. Chiefly did he delight to paraphrase some portions of the lively oracles, directly from the original, warlike or peaceful, as his mood might suggest. Judge for yourselves, as I read his beautiful version of Psalm xxiii., whether the strains of our Barak, sung during the intervals, and near the close, of his long conflict, shall be allowed to sleep in oblivion:

Jesus, Jehovah—Savior, stands,
  Shepherd and Bishop of my soul;
His thoughtful love, his mighty hands,
  My wants supply, my foes control.

In shady meadows, fresh and green,
  Where softly purling water flows,
While noonday showers her arrows' sheen,
  He grants me a divine repose.

Whene'er I wander from the fold,
  With patient toil he seeks for me,
In deserts drear, or mountains cold,
  And sets my soul at liberty.

To prove his tender shepherd care,
  And guard me that no more I stray,
With hands of love and holy fear
  He leads me, in his own right way.

What though it run through death's dark vale,
  I walk—whatever may betide,
Though hellish shapes and sounds assail—
  Walk, fearless, at my Shepherd's side.

Mid envious and malignant foes,
  Thou dost my table daily spread:
My cup with blessings overflows,
  And holy joy anoints my head.

Kind Shepherd—Savior! all my days
  Goodness and grace will follow me;
Safe in thy house I'll sing thy praise,
  And, lamb-like, I will follow thee!

Yet once more, listen to his muse, as it breathed
Æolian tones, a token already that his spirit was
pluming its wings to "fly and find rest." The poem
was composed the night after his last eloquent speech
before the Presbyterian Ministers' Association in Cincinnati, wherein he protested so earnestly against the
encouragement of public excitements, and the advocacy of innovations in the doctrine and order of the
Church, which seemed to him destructive of its very
foundations. Debates prevailed as to fundamental
theological truth, the emendation of the Standards,
the authority of the common faith of the Church, the
encroachment of a female ministry, the permanent of-
ficial tenure of the active eldership, an irresponsible
unlicensed ministry, and fanatical measures of moral
reform. He looked around him and all was stormy.
The world was agitated. He looked to the Church,
and beheld murmuring and division arising, notwithstanding boasted external reunion and promised peace.
He looked within at his own soul, and still the
struggle with sin went on. He turned, as the minstrel
of Israel turned, to Him who pities the suppliant, and
hears the suppliant's moan. He sighed for rest. He
prayed:

O Father of mercies, of holiness, harmony, peace!
  From a world of apostasy, sorely by Satan opprest,
Despairing, I lift up mine eyes to the kingdom of bliss;
  O give me the wings of a dove! I would fly and find rest.

From the waters of Noah the wanderer turned to the ark,
    And pleadingly knocked at the window with fluttering breast;
So might I, too, escape from a life—sea so dreary and dark—
    O give me the wings of a dove! I would fly and find rest.

An ocean, tempestuous, swept by the wild winds of heaven,
    Shadowed forth to the prophet earth's fierce population unblest;
The tempest still rages, the sea to its center is riven;
    O give me the wings of a dove! I would fly and find rest.

The group of Laocoon, type of humanity stands,
    Sin and death, twin constrictors, rear high their cerulean crest
O'er father and children, begirt by their horrible bands;
    O give me the wings of a dove! I would fly and find rest.

Thy Church, blessed Lord, once a kingdom of love, joy, and peace,
    Distracted, discordant, by faction and folly possessed,
No solace supplies to the spirit that sigheth for ease;
    O give me the wings of a dove! I would fly and find rest.

Coming home to my heart, to the kingdom of heaven within,
    By native depravity, open transgression, distressed,
Crest-fallen, I cry, in this life and death struggle with sin,
    O give me the wings of a dove! I would fly and find rest.

But, patience, my spirit! thy service and discipline o'er,
    Borne upward by angels to dwell in the realms of the blest,
This wail of the sin-stricken soul thou shalt utter no more:—
    " *O give me the wings of a dove!*" Thou *shalt* fly and find rest.

What shall I say in praise of this perfect production? *Palmam, qui meruit, ferat!* " Let him, who has deserved it, bear the palm!" Our Barak could not only sweep the strings of a David, but play as sweetly on a harp of his own.

The times in which Dr. Thomas lived, taken together, were an epoch-making period in the history of the Church and the nation. The influence of the mighty revival movement, during the close of the last century and the beginning of the present, was felt throughout that whole generation in which, as a young man, he began his career. He was himself part of the golden fruit sprung from those precious outpourings of the Spirit of God, when such men as Spring and Skinner, Griffin and McDowell, Barnes, Brainerd, Janeway and Nevins, Tyng, Fuller, Wilson, Plumer, Breckinridge, Duffield, Baker and McIlvaine, were proclaiming the gospel from hearts fired with zeal for the salvation of souls, and building up the American Church which now overshadows the land from north to south and from east to west. In those days the house of God was made awful by reason of the presence of the Lord. Revival was the rule, indifference the exception. Hundreds and thousands were gathered into the gospel net during those times. Convicted sinners, pricked in their hearts, used to rise in the sanctuary, hundreds at once, and stand for the prayers of God's people. Undreamed of wonders were beheld through the opened windows of heaven, the showers coming down not only in their season, but continuing to water the hill of Zion, and make the places round about a blessing.

But while God prepares His Church for blessing, and imparts the same, Satan ever seeks to counteract it, in some measure, by the folly of men. It was so, especially, in the times to which we refer. Enthusiasts took occasion from the presence of high religious fervor to make human feelings and excitements, apart from the divine word, the standards and rules of human duty. Providence, fancied light in the mind, and religious impressions, together with a zeal for God not according to knowledge, were practically co-ordinated with the revealed word of God, as sufficient guides for Christian action. New measures, unsupported by scriptural warrant, were introduced into many of the churches, giving rise to contentions both in doctrine and order. The natural ability of lost man began to be magnified in reaction against the true conception of the sovereignty of divine grace. Preachers, too, self-sent, and self-authorized, began to roam abroad, assuming an authoritative proclamation of the gospel, without responsibility for their teaching or their manners, to any spiritual court. From public halls they passed, at last, into the churches. The authorized ministry itself, influenced by the spreading leaven, gave countenance to the encroachment of disorder. The result is too well known. The Presbyterian Church was divided. Yet this was not all that entered into the history of that result. Side by side with the religious movement of the times, strange as it may seem, a grievous departure in the Church from the old sentiment of the fathers, in reference to the perpetuation of domestic slavery, took place. With this change of sentiment the period of violent pro-slavery and anti-slavery agitation commenced. The political affected the ecclesiastical, and division in the State contributed to effect a division in the Church.

It was during such a time as this it pleased God to call into His kingdom our departed brother. His public life spanned the whole measure of the great predominating slavery contest, when the voices of such men as Mason and Calhoun, Benton and Clay, Adams and Webster, Garrison and Giddings, Seward, Sumner and Wilson, were lifted in high debate, in the national councils. They were the times of gag-law, riot and mob, slavery extension, bloody atrocities and compromise, fugitive slave law, and Kansas outrage, the assertion of State sovereignty over Federal authority, and, in turn, of Federal usurpation over State constitutional enactment. He had lived to see the prisons of Ohio made traps to secure the rendition of the fugitive, and deeds of barbarity perpetrated in free States, by special police, at the remembrance of which humanity shudders. He had lived to see civil and political ostracism reflected in ecclesiastic courts and manners, and the sentiment of society brought to bear adversely, in Church and State, upon every man who dared to lift his voice in favor of the freedom of the slave. He had lived to see his own denomination thrice sundered, and every political party in the land, as well as almost every evangelical denomination, broken in twain by the destructive conflict. He lived to hear at length the trumpet of war sound " to arms," and to pass through a struggle which cost the nation the blood of 500,000 men and an expenditure of 3,000,- 000,000 of treasure. He lived to see slavery destroyed, the flag of the nation raised in proud triumph over every State in the Union, and the sundered branches of the Presbyterian Church reunited, save where the demand is still made that the Northern Assembly shall crave pardon of the South for the sin of its loyal deliverances.

As to the manner in which our brother deported himself in reference to the characteristics of this whole eventful period, his life was a bright testimony. The baptism of the Spirit, received upon his entrance into public life, remained with him to the last. The sacred fire never went out. Many were the revivals of religion in which he labored with the zeal of an apostle, drinking an abundant blessing to his own soul, while made a means of abundant blessing to others, watching ever for the early and the latter rain, and in times of drought, supplicating, like the prophet on Carmel, for the torrent from heaven. With new measures whether in doctrine, order, or worship, he had no sympathy. To an unauthorized and intermittent ministry he gave no sanction whatever, maintaining that consecration to the work of reconciling sinners to God demanded the most solemn and careful preparation, and the utmost unintermitting devotion. Fancied light apart from the word of God, and supposed to be received by prayer, he considered a delusion. In the words of Calvin, he held that "God has determined, indeed, that the Church should be guided by the Spirit, but yet has connected this guidance always with the word of God, that there may be no danger, or wavering, or uncertainty, and that the Church must have for its basis in all things the word of God, and not rest in general impressions of the Holy Spirit; that without the word of God, a man fluctuates to and fro with the Holy Spirit, and is in danger of becoming any thing, and that we bring division only on ourselves, for this, that we sin against the Holy Ghost, the builder of His own Church, by dividing Him from His own word, it being not less injurious to boast of the Spirit without the word than to appeal to the word as uninspired." As to making the providence of God the interpreter of Church and Christian duty, in contravention of the revealed will of God, he planted himself upon the common rule accepted by the Church in all ages, viz: that the providence of God can never be a light to the Church as against the written word of God. I know of no better expression of his views upon this point than the words of Milton, who said: "If it be affirmed that God, as being Lord, can do what He will, yet must it be said that God hath no will contrary to His own order, or what he hath already established in His own Church. The ways of Providence we adore and search not, but His revealed word is His will, His complete, His evident, His certain will. Herein He appears in human shape, binds Himself to His own prescriptions, and binds us beside to the same." How fully Dr. Thomas carried out these views in every-day life, on all social and public occasions, and enforced them as against the innovations which, in his view, threaten the Church at the present time, all his brethren who knew him can bear witness.

As to the question of slavery he was one of the foremost and most pronounced men of his time. From his youth he threw his whole energy and heart into the scale of freedom, and bared his breast to all manner of insult, proscription, obloquy and reproach. He took prominent part in the anti-slavery conventions that characterized the agitations of the period. Files of newspapers still exist, and living witnesses still arise, to remind us of the printed declarations that " a young preacher named Thomas and a young lawyer named Chase are expressing such dangerous sentiments regarding the abolition of slavery that they ought to be put down!" Christian men still exist who remember when every church in Cincinnati was closed against " the young preacher Thomas," save one. Let the mantle of oblivion forever cover the shame! Thank God, he lived to see the day when every church in Cincinnati would welcome his entrance to its pulpit, and admiring audiences hang in rapture on his tongue! He lived to see the Rev. E. D. MacMaster, one of the

greatest of living theologians, ecclesiastically cut down
by his side, and driven by Southern influence from his
post of usefulness and labor. Let the mantle of oblivion cover, too, the enormity of that disgrace. What
cared either of these heroes for popular favor or popular reproach? Each could say, as did the dauntless
Chrysostom: "Let the enemy saw me in sunder I
have Isaiah before me! Let them plunge me into the
fiery furnace, I see the three Hebrew children wrapt
in the flames. If they give me to wild beasts, Daniel
was in the lion's den. Would they stone me? Stephen,
the proto-martyr, is my example. Would they bid for
my head? John Baptist is before me. Let them take
all I have. Naked came I into the world." Both
endured their reproach for the Master's sake, waiting
in hope for the day that should crown their believing
expectation—a day that came to them at last amid the
acclamations of a delivered Church, and the pæans of
a nation jubilant with songs of victory.

By some Dr. Thomas has been called "austere." If
by austerity is meant a lack of gentle and loving dis-
position, the charge is a sad mistake. If by austerity
is meant uncompromising and incorruptible integrity,
moral heroism in face of opposition, obloquy and
reproach, then it is a compliment to his Christian fidelity, a glory whose brilliance shall never pale in the
luster of his bright reputation. He lived in times of
social, civil and ecclesiastical demoralization. So
Elijah and John the Baptist were austere. So the
prophets and judges of Israel were austere. So Calvin, and Luther, and Knox, and Melvill, and Milton,
and Cromwell, and the Hampdens, and Sidneys, and
Pyms, abroad in the panoply of the gospel and in the

majesty of popular rights, were austere. So Christ, the Master, was called "austere." To say that the corrupt times in which Mr. Thomas lived stood in awe of him, is beautifully to crown him with honor. So corrupt Israel stood in awe of the seraphic Ezekiel, the tearful Jeremiah. So Sisera stood in awe of Barak, Midian of Gideon, and the confederate kings of Canaan before Joshua on the heights of Beth-horon. Your neutrality man, " neither hot nor cold," " the gentleman from Laodicea," as our departed brother was wont to baptize him, he could not endure. Dr. Thomas was no man to trifle with high moral issues, nor with insipid obsequious and polite circumlocution, simper out with a French smile, " My dear Mr. Elymas, it may be possible, perhaps, that peradventure you are laboring somewhat under the difficulty of a slight misapprehension." None of this. But. Paul-like, " O full of subtilty, and all mischief, thou child of the devil, thou enemy of all righteousness, wilt thou not cease to pervert the right ways of the Lord?" Sin was sin to him, and he hated it with a perfect hatred. He remembered the woes his Master had denounced, not only over Bethsaida and Chorazin, but made echo in the priest's court, in the temple of Jerusalem. Whether the object of his attack was slavery or popery, infidelity or intemperance, false science or false legislation, the bar-room or the theater, a corrupt pulpit, press, society, or worldly pleasure—loving Christianity, he was " no respecter of persons." Faithful among so many faithless, unbought, unsold, he kept his garments clean. Manliness, Christian heroism, this was the virtue that shone untarnished through all the rest, untarnished, bright as the sheen of the sun.

Be this thy crown, brave soldier of the cross,
That what men counted gain, thou only loss,
Be this thy glory, thy undying fame,
That incorruptible is written o'er thy name.

Shall I tell you the secret of our brother's life, so
manly and true, so courageous and noble ? It was faith
in God. This magic spring, once touched, reveals to us
the hidden Christian workings of his soul, and explains
the grandeur of all his public acts. It was this divine
virtue which, unknown to the "fearful and unbeliev-
ing," has ever been to the brave their inspiration in the
hour of danger, and to the feeble their strength in every
conflict. By it he stood, walked, ran, wrestled, fought,
endured, overcame, lived, died, and entered heaven.
" He believed God." He " conferred not with flesh and
blood." He declared "the whole counsel of God."
It was the measure of his ·Christian greatness. The
object from which its power was derived was not any
mere abstract idea of duty or law, right or wrong,
fluctuating and powerless, but the living, personal God
Himself, in Christ, and so, next to God, his faith became omnipotent. It could master all things. It was
no mere opinion; it was not an intellectual act alone,
but a moral act as well, an act which became, no less
than a habit, the synthesis of reason, heart, and will, in
their spiritual efflorescence, the plural unit in consciousness, of spiritual knowledge, confidence, and
self-surrender, so that to " believe " was to "know," and
" to know," " to believe," and both to " follow." The
Holy Ghost, thus grasping his whole intellect, sensibil-
ity, and will, in one divine renewal, made his whole
inward spiritual life a "life of faith on the Son of
God," in thought, feeling, volition, and his whole outward life a life of " obedience even unto death." Hence

his trials; hence his struggles; hence his unflinching perseverance and glorious victory. So was it with the "elders" of Israel. Many virtues each possessed as peculiar, but this one, common and pre-eminent among all. Here is the central gem, more brilliant than all the rest, shining in the crown of their fame, and brightening as the ages wear away. It was this practical and elementary principle, this living power, which underlaid the whole Christian life of our brother, and preserved his moral aspect firm while others changed their Proteus-face, this conserving virtue which in any soul, or any people, is their moral life and health, but which, once lost, the soul, the church, the nation, rots like some base carcass, fit only for the eagle's beak, or to be hidden out of sight.

By this divine virtue were all the victories of old. By it Abel "obtained witness that he was righteous," Enoch that "he pleased God," Noah that he should be "heir of the righteousness of faith," and Abraham that in his seed "all the nations of the earth should be blessed." By it Moses rejected, like our brother, offered greatness, "esteeming the reproach of Christ "greater riches than the treasures in Egypt, "choosing to suffer affliction" because he had "respect to the recompense of the reward." By it Gideon brake the lamps and pitchers in the camp of the Midianites and routed their affrighted host. By it Barak swept down from the summit of Tabor, with Deborah at his side, and "led captivity captive" on the plain of Esdraelon. It was the faith of Samson who smote, one day, a thousand Philistines "with the jaw-bone of an ass," and of Shamgar, left-handed, who, another day, smote six hundred more "with an ox-goad." It inspired the Gileadite valor of Jephthah who "smote the Ammon-

ites from Aroer to Minnith, even twenty cities ; " the
faith which in righteous Samuel " hewed Agag in
pieces before the Lord; " which in Hezekiah became
" strength out of weakness; " which in Joshua and
David " escaped the edge of the sword," and " turned
aliens to flight"—Og, king of Bashan, Sihon, king of
the Amorites, Oreb and Zeeb, Zebah and Zalmunna, and
sent them, whirling, like thistle-down, in the air, before
the hurricane's blast. In Daniel and his companions it
" stopped the mouths of lions and quenched the violence of fire." It was the faith of Paul, and of John,
and of Christ Himself—the faith of martyrs, confessors, reformers, and saints in all ages, who have run
their race, and fought their fight, " looking unto
Jesus."

Nor, in closing this imperfect portrait of our departed brother, could I do better than, imitating an
inspired precedent, emphasize, in a brief enumeration,
some of the victories of his own faith, whereby, like
. elders in other days, he approved himself unto God,
and " obtained a good report."

By faith it was that, in 1831, when nineteen years
old, he " fled for refuge to lay hold on the hope set before him in the gospel," and committing body and
soul to Jesus, as to a faithful Creator and living Redeemer, laid, by this one act, the foundation of all his
future victories over self, sin, the world, Satan, death,
the grave, and hell !

By faith, in 1836, when twenty-four years old, he
began to " preach the unsearchable riches of Christ "
to dying men, and in the blessing which crowned his
faithful ministry of forty years obtained witness that
he was " a chosen vessel " to turn men " from darkness
to light, and from the power of Satan unto God."

By faith, in 1843, when only thirty-one years old, he encountered in debate, during the September Sessions of the Synod of Cincinnati, at Hamilton, the President of Miami University—now singing hallelujahs beside him in glory—who, during nine hours, defended the proposition that the apostle, in 1 Timothy vi. 1–5, uses the term *"yoke"* to indicate New Testament countenance of involuntary and perpetual slavery, and, in an impromptu response of five hours, lifting his voice like a trumpet, blew upon his antagonist the inspiration of the Holy Ghost in Isaiah lviii. 6, commanding the oppressor to "undo the heavy burdens, to let the oppressed go free, and to *break every yoke!*" And by faith, when threatened with riot and mob-law in his ministry, he lifted his voice only the louder.

By faith, in 1846, when thirty-four years old, he stood with the now sainted Fullerton, of Chillicothe, in the General Assembly, in Philadelphia, and contended against almost the entire body, for principles of righteousness, now received without question by the whole Northern Church, and gave evidence, as an eminent survivor declares it, that both "he and his friend were fearfully and wonderful in earnest."

By faith, in 1849, when thirty-seven years old, he assumed the duties of the Presidency of Hanover College, in an eventful crisis, all eyes being turned to him for succor, and all hands outstretched to welcome him, and four years later was inducted into his chair in New Albany Seminary, and, later still, in Lane Seminary, challenging, in these three institutions, the admiration of colleagues and directors, for his integrity and zeal, and leaving behind him a multitude of pupils who mourn his loss, and cry after him as they gaze on his bright ascension, "My father! my father! the chariot of Israel and the horseman thereof!"

By faith, in 1859, when forty-seven years old, he despaired not, when beholding his brave colleague cut down on the floor of the General Assembly by voices and votes of Southern sentiment, but declared that God would yet exalt his head, which God did, triumphantly, seven years later, in 1866, when, with Assembly acclamation, he was borne to the very chair from which, seven years before, he had been driven by a Church in chains to slavery.

By faith, in 1861, when forty-nine years old, he lifted his manly voice in the General Assembly, at Philadelphia, protesting against the effort there made to commit the Presbyterian Church to silence, in that hour when treason unsheathed its sword against the national government, and the blood of brethren in the same fold was soon to flow in streams, either to terminate or extend and " conserve " the system of American slavery.

By faith, in 1866, when fifty-four years old, he stood upon the platform of the General Assembly at St. Louis—notable forever in the history of the Church—and delivered upon the exciting issues of that hour, a speech the vibrations of which still tingle in the memory of all who heard it, an impromptu effort carrying the house by storm, and which, could European Liberators and Reformers have matched it, would have won them the honor of being drawn in laureled triumph through the streets.

By faith, in 1873, when sixty-one years old, and his hairs had begun to silver for the tomb—rich in the experience of many a conflict, yet richer in the enjoyment of communion with his Lord—he was able to say, in calm review of all his struggles, trials, and whole Christian life, " I gave myself to Christ forty-two years

ago. From the hour of my first confidence in Christ
.I have never doubted His interest in me, nor mine in
Him!"

By faith, in 1874, when sixty-two years old, over-
borne by accumulated labors—weary of the " life and
death struggle with sin," longing for " home" and
sighing to " fly away and find rest "—he rallied his
drooping spirit, and, drawing comfort from the promise
of Christ to find him a place in heaven, woke his muse
to sing, and his harp to breathe its last sweet min-
strelsy :

O Guardian Savior! who hast led
My steps from earliest infancy,
Thou hadst not where to lay Thy head,
Yet Thou hast found a place for me!

And when my spirit wings her flight,
I dare not doubt that I shall see,
In worlds of everlasting light,
The promised HOME prepared for me.

And so, by faith, in 1875, when sixty-three years
old—his course nearly run—he calmly called to his
side his sons one day, saying to each, "Give me your
hand, my son; kiss me!"—still concealing in his heart
the consciousness of his approaching departure. And
so, shortly after, leaving the wife of his youth and his
dear surviving ones to struggle on a little longer in
this world of sin, he closed his eyes and fell asleep in
Jesus.

Leave Leonidas to his glory at Thermopylæ! Admire
the greatness of Epaminondas who refused to let the
spear be drawn from his side till the shout of Theban
victory rang in his ears! Their laurels fade before
those of our Barak, who, during a whole generation,
stood in the moral breach till conquest bore him in
triumph to his reward.

Farewell, brave soldier of the cross! Thou art gone to banquet with comrades in arms gathered from all ages around the table of thy great Captain—with patriarchs and prophets, judges and kings, apostles and the Master himself—with martyrs, reformers, confessors and saints, whose robes are "made white in the blood of the Lamb"—with bright "stars" in that "cloud of witnesses" whose trailing galaxy reveals the face of thine own Fullerton, and of the sainted MacMaster who said, with his dying breath, "*I have fought a good fight; I have finished my course; I have kept the faith!*" Blessed company ye are! What beauty blooms upon your countenances, ye veterans of the Lord, once so worn with care! What smiles! What happiness! That crystal river! Those palms and golden crowns! That multitude of "the spirits of just men made perfect!" That song of victory in which the angels join! That Paradise of God! And thou—*Thomas Ebenezer Thomas*—could human breasts be laid open for inspection, thy image would be found, here graven as with the point of a diamond! Dead, yet speaking, thy voice shall still be heard saying, "This is the way, walk ye in it!" The memory of thy light, as it set below our western horizon, shall long leave within us the wake of its brightness, to gild our pathway to the tomb! As we follow thee to thy rest, thy example shall still inspire us to emulate the deeds thy faith has made immortal!

Peaceful be the slumber of thy mortal remains! White sentinels, unseen, watch the dust that is precious in the sight of God. Yet a little while, and "the trumpet shall sound," and "the dead in Christ shall rise first," and we, and thou, and thine, and the whole Church of God, shall meet to be severed again, never, forevermore! Together we shall survey the past, recount the dangers of the way, and sing the victories of faith.

And, now, unto Him who created thee, renewed thee, endowed thee, tried thee, sustained thee—who gave thee, took thee, and soon will restore thee—to Him, the Shepherd of the sheep, the First-begotten from the dead, Prince of the kings of the earth and Captain of salvation, be all glory and honor, and power and majesty, and might and dominion, in all the churhes, and throughout all the world, both now and forever. Amen and amen!

The dead are like the stars by day.
  Withdrawn from mortal eye;
But, not extinct, they hold their way
  In glory through the sky.
Spirits, from bondage thus set free,
Vanish amid immensity!

Appendix.

AMONG the various written communications privately received from ministerial brethren, during the preparation of the preceding discourse, there are two whose contents deserve to be appended to the discourse itself, as part of the widespread tribute of affection spontaneously offered to the memory of the deceased. These communications are from the pens of Rev. J. M. Stevenson, D. D., of New York City, and Rev. S. F. Scovel, D. D., of Pittsburg, Pennsylvania. Acknowledgments are due, not only to these brethren, but also to Cyrus Falconer, M. D., of Hamilton, Ohio, Rev. George C. Heckman, D. D., President of Hanover College, Indiana, for written accounts of Dr. Thomas, and to Rev. A. A. E. Taylor, D. D., President of Wooster University, Ohio, Rev. J. G. Monfort, D. D., editor of the *Herald and Presbyter*, Rev. J. L. Evans, D. D., of Lane Theological Seminary, and others from whose published notices of Dr. Thomas, valuable facts have been drawn, and accuracy reached as to some important dates in his life. The memorial resolutions passed by the First Presbyterian Church, Dayton, the Seventh Presbyterian Church, Cincinnati, the Presbyterian Ministers' Association, Cincinnati, the Board of Trustees of Miami University, of which Dr. Thomas was so long a member, and by the colored people of Dayton, merit, though not here inserted, to be mentioned in company with the numerous testimonies of the press, both secular and religious, as part of the universal expression of sorrow and esteem, evoked by the death of Dr. Thomas. In addition to the papers of Drs. Scovel and Stevenson, the memorial actions of the Trustees and Faculty and students of Lane Seminary are appended, together with a brief notice of the funeral services. The memorial tribute of Cincinnati Presbytery, of which Dr. Thomas was a member at the time of his death, is also properly added.

FUNERAL OF DR. THOMAS.

The remains of Dr. Thomas were conveyed, by sorrowing friends, to their last resting-place in the public cemetery at Dayton, Ohio, on Friday, February 5, 1875. At nine o'clock of the morning, the ministers of the city of Cincinnati and suburbs, together with a large concourse of friends, met at the residence of the deceased, on Walnut Hills, near Lane Theological Seminary, to pay to the honored dead the tribute of their respect. The professors of the Seminary, and the whole body of students, were present. Appropriate services were conducted at the house by Rev. Hugh Smythe, pastor of the Seventh Presbyterian Church, Cincinnati, and Rev. J. G. Monfort, D. D., editor of the *Herald and Presbyter*. The pall-bearers were Rev. Dr. Evans, Professor in Lane Seminary, Dr. Worrall, pastor of the First Presbyterian Church, Covington, Kentucky, and Dr. West, pastor of the Lincoln Park Presbyterian Church, Cincinnati, and Elders W. W. Scarborough, of the Walnut Hills Church, Dr. James Taylor, of the Second Presbyterian Church, Cincinnati, and H. W. Hughes, of Glendale. At the conclusion of the preliminary services in the house, the remains were conveyed, by train, to the city of Dayton, where a relay of pall-bearers, chosen from officers and members of Dr. Thomas' last pastoral charge, were waiting to relieve those to whose care the remains had already been intrusted. They were borne from the depot to the First Presbyterian Church, a magnificent edifice erected by the liberality of the congregation during the pastorate of the deceased. As the coffin entered, the bell tolling, and passed through the main aisle to the bier, in front of the pulpit from which, so often, the eloquence of the deceased had streamed in other days, the tears and sympathies of the vast audience betrayed how deeply he had enshrined himself in the admiration and affections of the people. The vast massive edifice was thronged by mourners from all parts of the adjacent country. Hundreds of persons who came " to pay the last sad tribute " to the incomparable virtues of the deceased were unable to gain admittance. The great audience-room, the chapel, the vestibule, the hall, and all the approaches, were crowded to their utmost capacity. The services were tender, impressive and solemn. After an appropriate anthem by the choir, the Scriptures were read by Rev. Dr. Evans, of Lane Seminary. Prayer was offered by Rev. Dr. McKnight, of Springfield, Ohio. Rev. Dr. Worrall, of Covington, Kentucky, read the hymn commencing with the words :

"There is a land of pure delight."

After the singing of which, by the congregation, Rev. Dr. Smith, of Lane Seminary, delivered the funeral sermon from the words of the dying Savior, recorded in Luke xxiii. 46: "Father! into thy hands I commend my spirit," a discourse full of comfort, pathos, and power. The concluding prayer was offered by Rev. Dr. West, of Cincinnati. The following beautiful hymn of Montgomery, printed on slips of paper and distributed through the house, was then read by Rev. O A. Hills, of the Central Presbyterian Church, Cincinnati, and sung by the congregation standing :

"Servant of God ! well done;
  Rest from thy lov'd employ;
The battle fought, the victory won,
  Enter thy Master's joy."

The voice at midnight came ;
  He started up to hear,
A mortal arrow pierced his frame;
  He fell, but felt no fear.

At midnight came the cry,
  " To meet thy God prepare !"
He woke—and caught his Captain's eye ;
  Then strong in faith and prayer,

His spirit, with a bound,
  Burst its incumbering clay ;
His tent, at sunrise, on the ground,
  A darken'd ruin lay.

The pains of death are past,
  Labor and sorrow cease,
And life's long warfare clos'd at last,
  His soul is found in peace.

Soldier of Christ! well done;
  Praise be thy new employ;
And while eternal ages run,
  Rest in thy Savior's joy.

The benediction was pronounced by Rev. Dr. Smith, of Lane Seminary, after which the large body of ministers in attendance first passed out, immediately followed by the congregation. The procession moved to the public cemetery where the last solemn service was performed in a most touching and impressive manner at the grave, by Rev. Dr. Skinner, pastor of the Second Presbyterian Church, Cincinnati.

The coffin of the deceased was richly ornamented and strown with flowers. A portrait of the deceased was hung beneath the pulpit in view of the congregation during the service. Near the coffin stood a sheaf of wheat, fully ripe. The scene was one not soon to be forgotten. It spoke in language not to be misunderstood, the high and loving appreciation in which the religious community held the life, character, services, and memory of Dr. Thomas.

TRIBUTE OF DR. SCOVEL.

Sketch of Dr. Thomas from 1849–1857.—Dr. Thomas was not only well known to the friends of Hanover College by general reputation, but had won their special admiration by the able and admirable address delivered at one of the commencements on " The Literary Merits of the Bible." When, therefore, death had bereaved the college, in July, 1849, of one whose short presidency had been signally blessed in improving the financial condition of the college, and accompanied by remarkable revivals, all eyes turned at once to Dr. Thomas, and all hands were stretched out to him. He came promptly, and seemed to bring his whole soul and matured powers to the work. In 1853 the Theological Seminary, at New Albany, having overtured the Assembly, and very properly dissatisfied with the response, resolved to continue its sessions, and in 1854 made an appeal to Dr. Thomas to come to its help. He brought with him students as well as qualifications, and labored with success as Professor of Church History and Hermeneutics, adding also occasional lectures on the Ministry and its Work. This continued until the second and final crisis of this seminary's history, beginning with the cessation of its sessions in 1857, and terminating in Chicago in 1859.

Having become much endeared by occasional ministrations to the Old School Church, in New Albany, he became stated supply for that Church, and from this relation removed to Dayton in 1859.

In all the relations of an active and broad life, Dr. Thomas was pre-eminently *manly*. There was no concealment of convictions and no pandering to prejudices. The instinct of justice was easily roused in him, and never failed to carry with it that blaze of indignation which proved its genuineness. He loved all good, and with equal positiveness hated all evil. Assumption and pretension were absolutely foreign to him. His integrity was secured, and made the more striking, by his simplicity. There was sincerity in the glance of his eye, the grasp of his hand, and the tone of his voice. Whether on great or small accasions, on the street or in his study, he was always the same genuine true-hearted man. His sympathies were quick and his emotions lively. The fountain of tears and the spring of laughter were very nearly on the same level with him. Without a touch of levity or unsteadiness, he was exquisitely mobile and sensitive to grave or gay. What a treasure it was when he opened his heart in tenderness, or his memory in anecdote, or gave play to bright association and wit. Such character made him almost the idol of young men. He was never inaccessible, and never inconsiderate. He was not weak, and did by no means always cry "bene, bene," but when he corrected us, it was easily seen that the offense gave pain and correction was no pleasant task. His religious experience, as far

as it became known to us, was that which belonged to such
a character. It was full of fervor, of enjoyment of God in
nature and mind and art, and of deep thought ; and found
honest and frank expression in private and public. In all
things and everywhere he was real, sterling, genuine; a man
whose memory must grow the more powerful for good *the
more sadly one learns to contrast him with the many who
are not like him.* He was honest, bold, fearless, sincere, and
sympathetic. His graces and his gifts alike came out in his
work.

As President, he came to a most difficult task, and never
shrank from toil in accomplishing it. The financial problem
pressed all the time in the form of supplying sala-
ries from an inadequate fund, and urging a half-interested
and struggling church to the work of building and endow-
ment. If there was error in anything of this nature, it was
the error of trusting too implicitly the promises made in the
most solemn manner by representatives of the church.
Along with this, Dr. Thomas entered quite as vigorously upon
efforts to uplift the standard of scholarship, to improve the
methods of teaching, to increase the library and apparatus
and cabinets. This would be expected from one so fond of
learning, and of thoroughness in it, and whatever difficulties
he encountered in this direction were unflinchingly met, and
all the success possible under the circumstances was won.
Administratively, Dr. Thomas endeared himself to every
honest man in the college, and made himself respected by
the worthless and bad. Resoluteness and tenderness were
always combined. Personal interviews were preferred to
public and stinging rebukes. Playful banter sometimes accomplished what scolding could not have secured. His flexible nature fitted easily into the exigencies of the situation.
He never emphasized amiss. An immorality found him
firm and fiery, or tender, according as rebellion or submission
marked the offender's deportment. He knew when to appeal
to the nobler thoughts always accessible in young men.
Once, when many of the best men of the college had been
led into signing a protest against the discipline of an offend-

er, I remember to have watched the tears trickle through the fingers that covered his face, while the morning prayer was being offered by another member of the Faculty. And then, what an appeal! The most thoughtless of us bent under the power of a great heart administering justice *for our good.*

As a teacher, Dr. Thomas was unsurpassed. He passed easily from department to department, appreciating thorough work and detecting shams everywhere. His method was varied, but always intelligible. Adhering to the text-book, it was only as the body adheres to the spinal column. He built up upon text-books the thoughts and feelings of the whole subject. No question ever found him off-guard, and none ever frightened him into an unwary decision or harsh reproof. Though not always, he used often the Socratic method, and brought the pupil by successive and unerring steps face to face with his former blunder, to his temporary confusion but permanent benefit. Wit and humor were used as lubricators and stimulants for attention. In the professional chair of the seminary, Dr. Thomas commended to all his pupils, by method and example, a conscientious thoroughness of investigation, and a fearless acceptance of the final results of sound interpretation. He was sincere in holding the authority of the word of God to be superior to that of creeds and councils. I heard him lamenting that the library was deficient in the "Fathers," and then turning, with that merry twinkle in his eye, to say in the same breath, "But we have the *Grandfathers.*" He had an enthusiasm for the grammar and the lexicon, as "the nearest doors into the mind of the Spirit."

And the impressions made by the man and the master were supplemented, perhaps surpassed, by those which he made upon us as preacher. Here *all* his varied powers and solid character combined. He was expository, but never tediously minute or over-critical. No matter how long his sermon, there was always an impression left that he saw yet much more in the subject. He was a model in freedom of action without a touch of violence, of fervor without a moment's loss of self-possession, of musical, rhythmical and expressive diction without a suspicion of any false arts of the rhetorician. His preaching was simply the man and the student, and the Christian, kindled into superlative and intense activity. I am sure he never had his equal in America in the peculiar precision of his expression, joined with flexibility and warmth. There are precise men who are cold, and warm men who are not precise. There are men who are sometimes both clear and warm, but they betray the marks of effort and diligence to appear, the one or the other. But with Dr. Thomas all was as natural as the easy flow of limpid water. The sincerity of his preaching was more evident to me than that of any man I have ever heard, not excepting Spurgeon. At times, when subjects of commanding interest opened before him, he seemed to forget, as most of his audience did, the limitations of time and endurance. In quiet summer afternoons, during his presidency, with the audience of young men seated solidly in front of him, with Robinson's Greek Harmony open in his hand, and a section of the Life of Christ under review, I have known him to hold the students and audience beyond an hour and a half, and leave them hungering for more. He could not but be fervent who taught so clearly and felt so deeply. Rarely was a whole sermon controversial, and rarely a whole sermon without some trenchant blow at unbelief or error. He knew the Papacy and hated it. And no conflict with error but seemed to settle him deeper in the truth. He was an oak, and gathered new life out of the storms. His imagination was vivid, but exquisitely discriminating and chaste. In all his powerful figures I never heard a gross one.

In short, as preacher of the everlasting gospel, he brought all his resources and all his powers, and all in the most perfect subjection and in their highest exercise, to the work of glorifying God and saving souls. Such, and so great, was our loved Dr. Thomas.

TRIBUTE OF DR. STEVENSON.

I think of my dear brother Thomas as a schoolmaster, a pastor, a professor, and a beloved friend, and in each of these I find illustrations of his *love for the right*, his *heroism in its defense*, his *warmth of domestic and social affection*, and his *breadth and strength of Christian character*. I first met Dr. Thomas in 1831–32 as a fellow-student at Miami University in the palmy days of that institution, when the venerable Dr. Bishop was its head, and Professors McGuffey, Scott, Armstrong and McCracken its active and honored teachers. Of the two hundred and more young men there, he stands before memory's eye now, as he then appeared, honest, earnest, vivacious, with a sturdy and compact body, a clear and perspicacious mind, and a devout and loving heart, which easily distinguished him from most of his companions. All loved him; few cared to meet him either in the struggles of the playground or in the debating hall, while all, of like mind, rejoiced to join him in the prayer-meeting and the " Society of Inquiry."

Two incidents of his college life I recall, as will many others, with special vividness. In 1833 the cholera, a far more dreaded scourge than now, made its sudden and deathful appearance at Oxford, and within the first few hours swept away several citizens. The students in the university were soon in a complete panic, and determined to leave in a body. The Faculty counseled calmness and delay, but the fright of the students was uncontrollable, and the entire body met in the chapel and discussed the duty of a rebellion against the authorities. A vote was soon reached, and only six names were found in the negative; of these six Bro. Thomas was one. He believed it right to obey the authorities, and he defended his convictions against an overwhelming and intolerant majority, with a true heroism which ever after characterized his life.

His ardent love for the truth and his deep emotional nature were signally illustrated by a very different state of circumstances at another time in his college life. In 1833 (I think it was) an unusual religious interest prevailed for months among the pious students. Daily prayer and conference meetings were held in recitation rooms, and smaller gatherings in students' rooms at nine o'clock at night, for weeks, and an intense religious fervor was developed, which left its impress upon not a few during all their subsequent lives. During these meetings Bro. Thomas fell into mental struggles and spiritual darkness, which were most distressing to his friends, and agonizing to himself. He saw the truth of God's justice, and the criminality of sin, but could not see the infinite mercy of Christ as applied to his own soul. His chosen friends among the students prayed with him and for him, daily and nightly, rising at midnight to walk away into the grove with him to plead for the light of God's countenance. So resolved was he to see the depths of sin in the heart of man, and therefore in his own heart; so determined to magnify the infinite holiness of God's law; so honest in the application of these truths to his own case, and yet so unable to appropriate atoning grace, that we often feared his reason would give way under the stress of his agony. He read and studied the word of God incessantly, and at length, in His time, God brought him forth into the full and joyful realization of his love in Christ Jesus. From that hour he was a bright, trustful, joyous, exultant Christian, such as he could never have been had God not led him through these depths of experience. That precious Bible was ever afterward the man of his counsel; and with the strength of his massive intellect, and the wealth of his ardent affections, he continued to teach and impress its sacred truths while he lived. The earnest biblical student, the profound scholar, the faithful pastor, the admirable teacher, which he became in turn, I doubt not received form and impress largely from this youthful struggle.

Of the nearly twenty-five years of Bro. Thomas' pastoral life, the record is in many thousand hearts.

During these years, in addition to a faithful, laborious and successful discharge of pastoral duty, he took a leading part in most of the questions which agitated the councils of the State and the courts of the Church.

He was almost THE FIRST, both in time and ability, in our Church, in the West, who thoroughly studied and manfully defended the right of the slave to freedom. In that long struggle for the right, in the early stages of which so little that is creditable to our philanthropy or Christianity appeared, Bro. Thomas always stood boldly for the truth, and with a strength of argument, and a fervor of rhetoric which few could equal, battled against the giant wrong of slavery, and this at times where it demanded a heroism equal to facing a cannon's mouth. On one occasion in the General Assembly, he and the now also sainted Rev. Hugh S. Fullerton, of Chillicothe Presbytery, stood, and for hours contended against the almost entire body, for principles of justice and righteousness which are now received without question by the entire Church, though their advocacy, then, led him to admit, and the Assembly to feel, that he was fearfully and wonderfully in earnest upon that question. He lived to see that truth which was " crushed to earth " many times in his person, " rise again," and the Church and the nation stand by his side in its maintenance.

After these earnest discussions in Synod or General Assembly, he would return to his pastoral duties and there resume the study of God's word with all the ardor and freshness of a new inspiration.

His ability and felicity in expounding the Holy Scriptures, whether with an isolated text or an entire chapter before him, none who ever heard him can forget. While exhibiting profound scholarship, and exhaustive analysis of most difficult passages, he combined simplicity of presentation and practicalness of application, so that the humblest hearer was edified under his ministry.

Nor did he limit his thoughts and sympathies to his own Church alone. As the representative of a great public, but not denominational institution (the American Tract Society), it was my privilege at various times to lay before Bro. Thomas, and his people, its modes of working for Christ.

Well do I remember how his great heart swelled, and his true catholicity of feeling welled forth, when he contempla· ted the vast work to be done in the evangelization of our country, and the zeal· and liberality essential for its accomplishment. While he devotedly loved the doctrines· of his own Church, his zeal for Christ was broader than denominational bounds, higher than church walls, and profound as the wants of the human soul. Hence he was prompt to labor for their salvation in all scriptural and approved methods.

It was during his last pastorate that the struggle for the nation's life occurred. Not only the members of his own congregation at Dayton, but the entire city, the State, the West, aye, the whole nation, know how promptly, fearlessly, persistently, eloquently, he contended for the integrity of the Union, and the freedom of those whose cause he had plead amid obloquy and scorn for so many years.

But in my opinion the art and science of teaching specially distinguished the public life of Dr. Thomas.· To this he devoted nearly fifteen of the forty years of his professional life ; more than two years in private schools, five as president of Hanover College, and seven as professor in the theological seminaries of New Albany and Lane.

As a director of Hanover College during his presidency, and pastor of the First Church of New Albany, during his session in that seminary, I was brought into most intimate relations with him, and speak from personal observation.

And here, his love for the truth—truth as against all superficialities and shams and half truths, or perverted and defective statements—was conspicuous and unvarying. No investigation was too protracted and exhausting, if at the end he attained the full conviction of having reached the bottom of the question. Days, weeks, months, he would pursue, with marvelous tenacity, a given line of study, and when it was mastered, the knowledge became a part of his mental being, ever after at hand for the instruction of others.

And then his enthusiasm and skill in imparting to his students, whether collegiate or theological, his wealth of

knowledge, were only equaled by his ability to set them
upon independent lines of study for themselves.

In all these respects he stood peer to the unsurpassed and
honored Dr. E. D. MacMaster, his associate and dearly loved
brother in New Albany Seminary. Can we doubt that they
now pursue their investigations together into the still higher
mysteries of the heavenly world?

Dr. Thomas, as Dr. MacMaster, bound his pupils to him as
intimate personal friends, as well as docile and earnest students. No ingenuous youth, once under his tuition, ever
ceased to honor and revere the teacher. Most especially was
this true of teacher and scholar in the study of the divine
word.

Here, the master's greatest power and warmest enthusiasm
were displayed, and here the pupil caught the fullest inspiration. Would to God that a mantle so fragrant of divine
truth, and so shining with light, might fall upon all the professors in our colleges and seminaries.

I may not close these few words in memory of our dear
Dr. Thomas without a distinct reference to his domestic and
social character. While seated with him and his intelligent
and lovely family under his ever hospitable roof, you forgot
the scholarly professor, in the warmth and unaffected simplicity of the genial and thoroughly human brother. Hap-
pily united with a cultured, amiable and obedient wife, and
with children gentle, loving and obedient, too, his home became a model Christian household. This home was always
for the husband and father a blessed resort when weary with
the cares and responsibilities of public station, or perplexed
with the exciting ecclesiastical or civil questions of the day;
and here he found his sure repose and sweetest rest. Within
this sacred circle came also, and because it was so sacred,
his sorest earthly trials. Death may enter some families and
break few bonds of affection, because few exist, but where
heart strings of husband and wife and children are all en-
twined, and the pulsations of every heart are in unison, let
but one babe be torn away from the circle, and the very
agony of dissolution seems to be suffered by all. Our de-

parted brother once and again was called to give up a dear child from his home, and here came out the amazing depth and strength of his personal affection.

As the pastor of his family, it was my sad duty to bury out of his sight a beautiful and precious boy, bearing his father's name, the darling "Ebenezer." Never did I see, in all my pastoral experience, so dreadful a struggle between pious resignation to the Divine Will, and overmastering parental love. But here, as in the other case, grace at length enabled him to say : "The *Lord* gave, and the *Lord* hath taken away. *Blessed be the name of the Lord.*"

And this large-hearted affection, which distinguished our brother in his family, was in due measure extended to his early associates of like character with himself, who in every instance, I venture to assert, were life-long friends. No engrossment in public duties, no separation by time and distance, no diversity of pursuits, or change of circumstances, ever alienated him from those he once loved. If they continued worthy of his affection, and especially if they served that Savior who had his supreme devotion, then were they always regarded as his friends in Christ Jesus. Nor is this trait of character to be lightly esteemed in a day when worldly ambition and narrow self-seeking alienate and embitter so many once bosom friends.

To sum up all in a few words, too few indeed, I recall Dr. Thomas, in his private life, as an affectionate husband, blessed with a loving and obedient wife, a loving father, blessed with dutiful children, a true friend and a devout Christian. In his public relations, as a noble patriot, a profound scholar, a successful teacher, an acute reasoner, an eloquent speaker, and a most instructive preacher. Not only his family and personal friends, but the Church and State have sustained a sad loss in the death of our beloved brother, Thomas Ebenezer Thomas. Blessed be God for his life, character, labors, and memory.

THE ACTION OF THE TRUSTEES OF LANE SEMINARY.

The Trustees of Lane Seminary, at their annual meeting,
May 13, 1875, entered upon their records the following
tribute to the memory of Dr. Thomas :

On the second of February, after nearly a year of conflict
with organic disease, Dr. Thomas Ebenezer Thomas was sud-
denly called, at the age of sixty-two, to lay aside his earthly
work forever. Both the pulpit and the press have already
recited his history and spoken eloquently of his abilities.
Struggling into manhood under peculiar embarrassments.
but made strong and sinewy by such struggles, he developed
during his earlier ministry both an unusual love of study and
culture, and also an active spirit of consecration to his
chosen work, which were the certain pledges of his future
eminence. Most of his active life was spent in the ministry.
and at Hamilton and Dayton, and elsewhere, he won for himself an extensive reputation as a prince among preachers.
Three times in his life, in Hanover College, in the Seminary
at New Albany, and in this institution. he was called to the
special task of educating young men chiefly for the ministry.
It was a work which he greatly enjoyed, and for which, especially in the department of biblical exposition, he had
some rare qualifications. In familiarity with the Scriptures
in the original tongues, in extensive acquaintance with com-
mentaries and expositions, in retentiveness of memory,
quickness of insight, and affluence of language, and in a certain spontaneous enthusiasm and aptness to teach, which
awakened responsive enthusiasm and responsive activity in
those whom he taught, he had few superiors. A student
rather than a man of affairs, and therefore less prominent in
ecclesiastical circles than he might have become, he was yet
remarkably earnest in his convictions. and prompt and fearless in action wherever he deemed it essential. Of slavery
and intemperance and other social evils, and of popery and
all other forms of priestly domination, he was from first to
last a resolute foe. Somewhat reserved toward strangers,
especially in later life, he was yet bright and vivid in com-

panionship, and warm and strong in his personal attach·
ments. His connection with this institution was compara-
tively brief, extending from the autumn of 1871 to his de-
cease, and limited, during the last year, by his physical
disabilities. His death at last was sudden, giving no oppor-
tunity for those expressions of personal faith and of interest
in the cause of Christ, which both his household and the
Church might have coveted, but of these his whole life gave
the best evidence. His remains are now resting on a beautiful slope consecrated to the dead. almost in sight of the
city, where, perhaps, the largest part of his maturer work
for the Master was done. There and here, and wherever he
lived and labored, his memory will long be cherished as that
of an assiduous student, an eminent preacher, and a devout
Christian man.

_____

THE ACTION OF THE STUDENTS OF LANE SEMINARY.

WHEREAS, In the providence of God we. the students of
Lane Seminary, have lost our beloved instructor, Dr. Thomas
E. Thomas,

Resolved, 1. That, in our judgment. the Church which he
dearly loved and labored for has sustained a loss which she
will long feel ; that the truth after which he was an ardent
seeker, and for which he contended against unnumbered foes.
has lost an able advocate; and the ministry of which he has
long been a devoted and successful member has lost a wise
father, a reliable counselor, and a sympathetic brother.

2. That the State in whose affairs he was ever interested
has lost an estimable and valued citizen. and the cause of
liberty an able and fearless defender.

3. That in the death of Dr. Thomas, Lane Seminary has sustained a great and severe loss, and the cause of Christian
learning a faithful and exceptional patron and example. The
Faculty have lost one who was an honor to their number and
a blessing to their fellowship. In this affliction, the students
of the seminary have sustained a loss which is peculiar and
irreparable. ' We shall ever remember his incomparable

qualifications as an instructor, his thorough integrity as a man, and his remarkable sincerity and devotion as a Christian. While we mourn his death we are thankful for his life and our acquaintance with him. To have known him was to love him. We shall honor his memory as that of a father and a friend.

4. That we, also sufferers in this affliction, extend heartfelt sympathy and condolence to the bereaved family and friends, and we commend them in faith and love to our Father in heaven and to the ward of His grace.

5. That a copy of these resolutions be sent to the family of the deceased, and that they be published in the press of Cincinnati and other cities.

ACTION OF THE PRESBYTERY OF CINCINNATI, APRIL 16, 1875.

Presbytery records the death of one of its most learned, honored and usful members, Rev. Thomas Ebenezer Thomas, D. D., Professor of New Testament Greek and Exegesis, in Lane Theological Seminary, which occurred on the second day of February, 1875. We tender to the family of our deceased brother our cordial sympathy, and our earnest desire that a covenant-keeping God will sustain and bless his bereaved widow and children in their painful affliction, and comfort them with the consolations of that precious gospel which he so dearly loved, and so efficiently commended by his life and labors. While we would reverently bow in submission to the will of God, who doth all things well, we would express our painful sense of the loss which this event brings to the Church of which our departed brother was a minister, so able, efficient and beloved, and to the school of the prophets, of which he was one of its most distinguished and successful instructors.

Oh! is it not a noble thing to die
As dies the Christian, with his armor on?
What is the hero's clarion, though its blast
Ring with the mastery of a world, to this?
What are all the searching victories of mind,
The lore of ages vanished? What are all
The trumpetings of proud humanity
To the short history of him who makes
His sepulcher beside. the King of kings?

www.ingramcontent.com/pod-product-compliance
Lightning Source LLC
Chambersburg PA
CBHW020245090426

42735CB00010B/1848